CGP has Phonics for Little Wandle sounded out!

CGP's Workbooks for Little Wandle are full of fun and friendly activities to build Year 1 pupils' confidence as they learn to read and write.

They follow the Little Wandle Letters and Sounds Revised programme exactly, so you can be sure they cover everything children need.

This is the **Year 1 Workbook** for **Spring Term**.
It covers the second part of **Phase 5** of the Little Wandle Programme, including:

- Alternative spellings of vowel and consonant sounds
- Tricky words

What CGP is all about

Our sole aim here at CGP is to produce the highest quality books — carefully written, immaculately presented and dangerously close to being funny.

Then we work our socks off to get them out to you — at the cheapest possible prices.

Contents

Editors: Aimee Ashurst, Claire Boulter, Helen Clements, Catherine Heygate, Kirsty Sweetman
With thanks to Ellie Canham, Emma Crighton and Juliette Green for the proofreading.
With thanks to Alice Dent for the copyright research.
ISBN: 978 1 83774 161 8

Printed by Elanders Ltd, Newcastle upon Tyne.
Based on the classic CGP style created by Richard Parsons.

How to Use this Book

This book is for children to complete in the Spring Term of Year 1.
It matches the Little Wandle phonics scheme.

The box at the top of the page contains instructions. Read through these with your child and go through the worked example so they know what to do.

This book requires your child to match pictures to words. You may need to help your child identify some pictures they're not sure of.

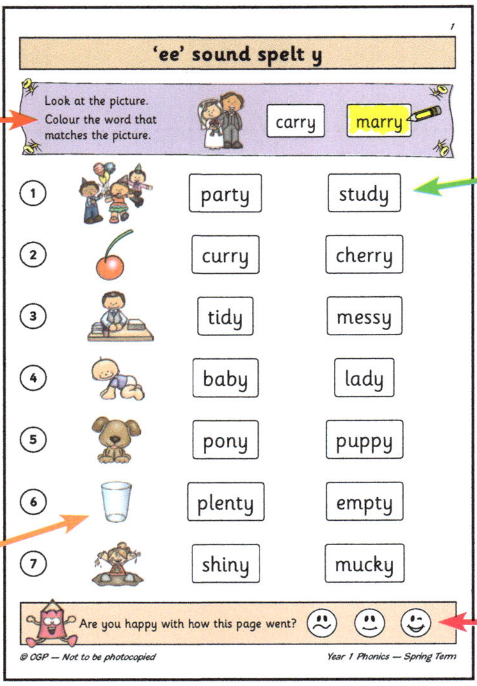
'ee' sound spelt y

Look at the picture. Colour the word that matches the picture. carry marry

1	party	study
2	curry	cherry
3	tidy	messy
4	baby	lady
5	pony	puppy
6	plenty	empty
7	shiny	mucky

Are you happy with how this page went?

© CGP — Not to be photocopied   Year 1 Phonics — Spring Term

Talk your child through the first question. Each question follows the same format, so encourage your child to tackle the remaining questions independently.

Your child can colour the self-assessment graphics to show how they got on with each page.

Phonics Hints for Helpers

- Pronunciation of some words will vary between different accents. If a child's accent doesn't follow the pronunciation suggested in this book they should practice reading the words in their own accent.
- A grapheme is a letter or group of letters that represents one sound.
- A digraph is a grapheme which uses two letters to represent one sound.
- A trigraph is a grapheme which uses three letters to represent one sound.
- A split vowel digraph is a digraph where the two letters of the grapheme are separated in a word. A curved line is used as a reminder that these letters are working together to make one sound.

- Word frames are used in spelling activities. There is usually one box for each grapheme (split vowel digraphs have two). Digraphs and trigraphs have wider boxes than single-letter graphemes.

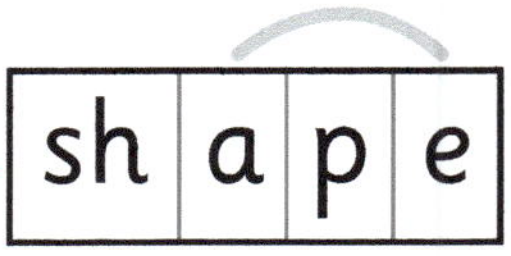

- Tricky words are common words which contain a sound that has not been learned yet. In some tricky words, the letters make a sound that does not correspond to the pronunciation children might expect.

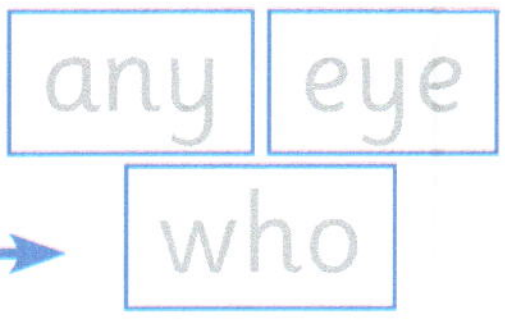

Scan the QR code for more information about phonics.
You can also find this information at:
cgpbooks.co.uk/rocket

Phonics Guide

'ee' sound spelt y

Look at the picture.
Colour the word that matches the picture.

carry | marry

1.  party | study

2.  curry | cherry

3.  tidy | messy

4.  baby | lady

5.  pony | puppy

6.  plenty | empty

7.  shiny | mucky

Are you happy with how this page went?

'e' sound spelt ea

In some words, the grapheme **ea** makes the sound in **head**. In others it makes the sound in **beach**.

Read the words. Draw lines to show which sound **ea** makes in each one.

head

beach

eats

1 weather

2 bread

3 clean

head

beach

4 thread

5 seal

6 heavy

7 speak

How easy did you find these questions?

'w' sound spelt wh

Look at the picture.
Use the graphemes
to make the word.

i wh k s

wh	i	s	k

1 

l wh ee

2 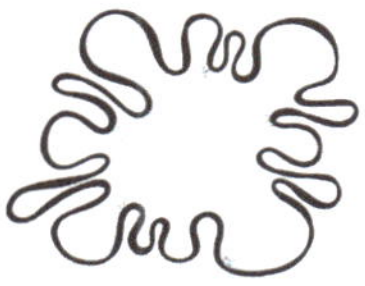

t wh i e

3 

wh l a e

4 

i wh s er p

5 

wh i k s er

Did you whizz through this page?

'oa' sound spelt oe and ou

Read each word.
Tick the word that contains the same sound as the grapheme in red.

cloak

goes ✔ 

noisy ☐

1 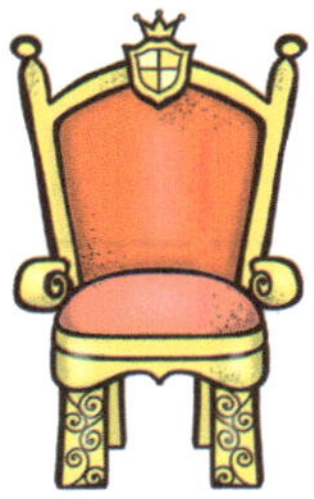 throne

socks ☐ 

toes ☐ 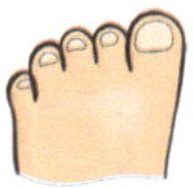

2 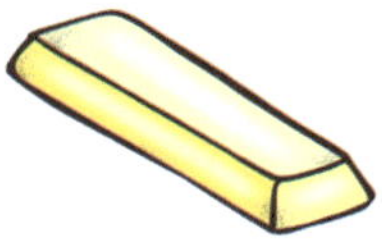 gold

rocket ☐ 

shoulders ☐ 

3  goat

woe ☐ 

joy ☐ 

4  globe

boulder ☐ 

flower ☐ 

How did this page go? Colour a face.

Tricky words

Trace the tricky words.
Then copy the right tricky word to complete each sentence.

He has not got | any | bread.

any   many   again

1. I saw so ______ whales.

2. Do you want ______ curry?

3. Joe had to start ______ .

4. It has so ______ heads!

5. Molly has hurt her shoulder ______ .

Did you have any trouble with this page?

Mixed practice

Read each sentence. Draw a line to match it to the best picture.

We tap our toes to any music.

1. A tiny fairy sat on the heavy boulder.

2. I butter the bread while Joe whisks the eggs.

3. Henry has so many party hats on his head.

4. Moe wants to ride the white pony again.

5. He only goes to rugby when the weather is sunny.

Are you happy with all these sounds?

'igh' sound spelt y

Read each word.

Then write each one under the sound that the grapheme **y** makes.

cry

'igh' sound

cry

1. fly 
2. funny 
3. sticky 
4. reply 
5. berry 
6. happy 
7. spy 
8. why 

'igh' sound		'ee' sound	

Were you flying on this page?

'oa' sound spelt ow

Read the words.

Colour the word where the grapheme **ow** makes the 'oa' sound.

brow

scowl

show

1 brown | gown | blown

2 cow | mow | bow

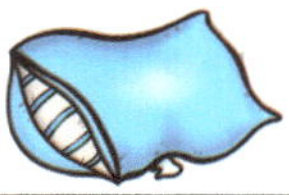

3 pillow | owl | growl

4 wow | grow | how

5 slower | shower | flower

Did you get into the flow of this page?

'j' sound spelt g

Read the word.
Colour the picture that matches the word.

cage  

1 gem  

2 magic  

3 pages  

4 huge  

5 stage 

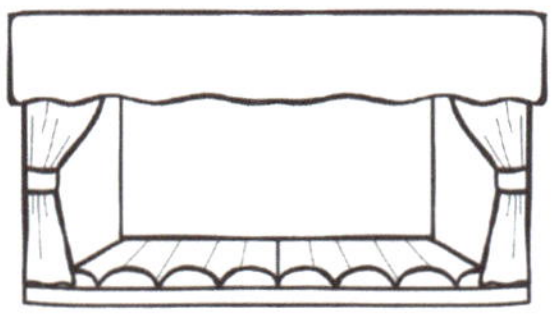

6 gingerbread  

7 danger  

 Do you feel like a genius after this page?

'f' sound spelt ph

Read each word.
Tick the word that contains the same sound as the grapheme in red.

fish — dolphin ☑ / shrimp ☐

1.  elephant

   frog ☐ 

   tiger ☐ 

2.  fairy

   dash ☐ 

   triumph ☐ 

3.  trophy

   shelf ☐ 

   chair ☐ 

4.  traffic

   phonics ☐ 

   snow ☐ 

Phew! Another page done — how was it? ☹ ☺ ☺

Tricky words

Trace the tricky words.
Then copy the right tricky word to complete each sentence.

I have | two | cats.

who | whole | where | two

1. ______ owns the house?

2. ______ is my phone?

3. Steph saw ______ giants.

4. My ______ team is in the photo.

5. ______ saw the sky glowing?

Was that a whole lot of fun?

Mixed practice

Read the question.
Then tick the box next to the correct answer.

Who owns two phones?		
	Sophie Sloth	☐
	Ralph Rabbit	☑

1. Where is Gemma?

- in a pigsty ☐
- in the snow ☐

2. Who has lots of energy?

- Deepa Dolphin ☐
- Phil Butterfly ☐

3. Who owns the magic beans?

- Saleem Spy ☐
- Gerry Giant ☐

4. Who will fry a whole fish?

- Robin Rat ☐
- Steph Slug ☐

5. Where is the arrow flying?

- in the sky ☐
- by two crows ☐

Are you glowing after this page?

'l' sound spelt le

Look at the picture.
Use the graphemes
to make the word.

e le tt k

k	e	tt	le

1 

t le t ur

2 

s dd a le

3 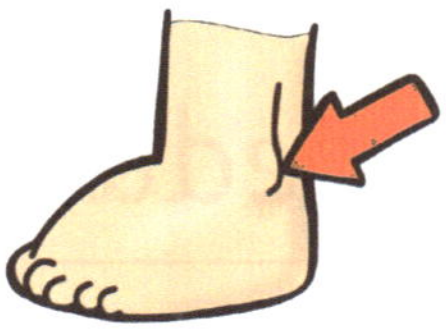

le nk a

4 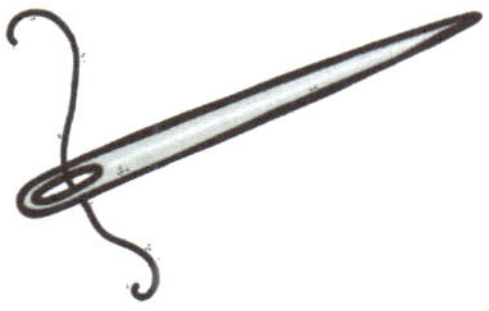

n ee le d

5 

a le c n d

How did you handle this page?

'l' sound spelt al

Look at the picture.
Colour the caption that matches the picture.

a royal mouse	a funny beetle

1 

boil a kettle	win a medal

2 

yellow petals	purple flower

3 

jump the hurdle	push the pedals

4 

her loyal puppy	his giant eagle

5 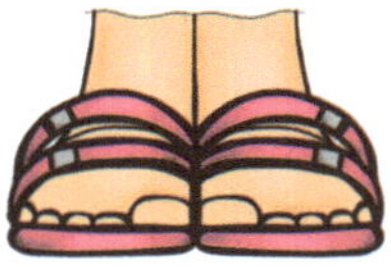

two brown buckles	two pink sandals

Are you totally happy with this page?

's' sound spelt c

Read the words.

Draw a line to match each word to the best picture.

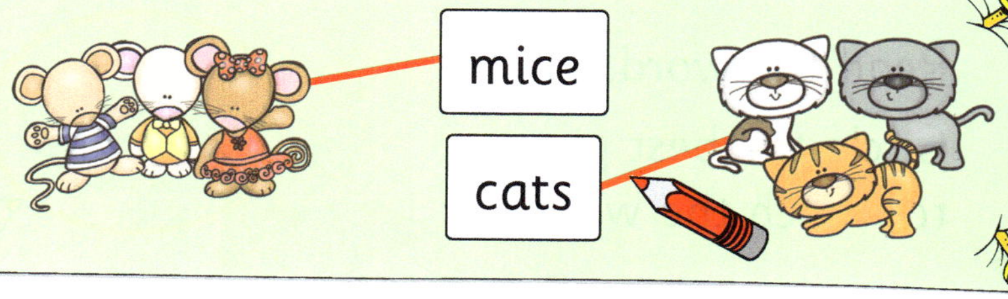

1

slice

cake

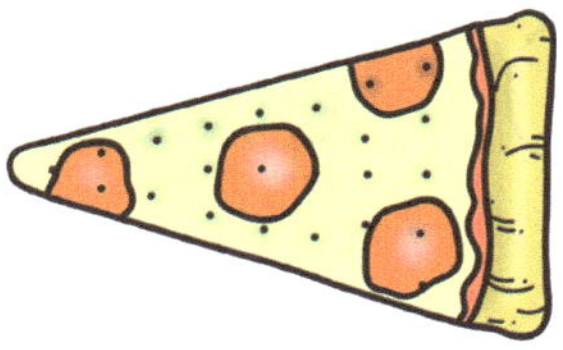

2

race

crawl

3

cube

circle

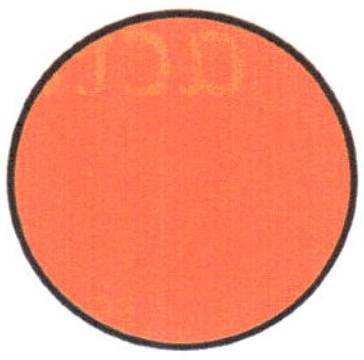

4

unicorn

princess

Was this page a piece of cake?

'v' sound spelt ve

Read the word.
Circle the best picture
to match the word.

massive

1	give		
2	leave		
3	curve	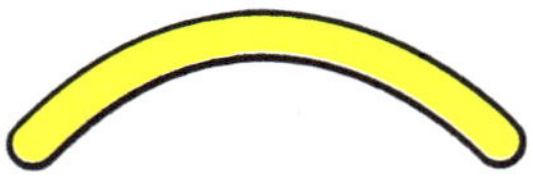	
4	active		
5	twelve	3	12
6	carve		

Did you love this page? Colour a face.

Tricky words

Trace the tricky words.
Then copy the right tricky word to complete each sentence.

I	call	to Tracy.

school   call   different

1. We have ______ apples.

2. Nancy races to ______ .

3. My uncles are so ______ .

4. Grace made a phone ______ .

5. Marshal wins a medal at ______ .

Did you find any of these words difficult?

Mixed practice

Read the sentence. Then write it on the dotted line.

We cannot solve this puzzle.

We cannot solve this puzzle.

1. I can juggle different things.

....

2. We leave school at twelve.

....

3. I give Coral the final slice.

....

4. I will call this beetle Stacy.

....

Did you handle this page well?

'u' sound spelt o-e, o and ou

Underline the '**u**' sound in each word.
Then write out all the different graphemes for the '**u**' sound that you have found.

country

none

1 come 

2 won 

3 couple 

4 brothers 

5 worry 

6 glove 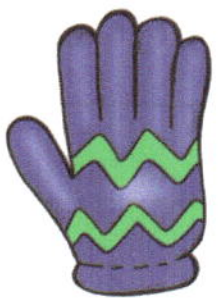

7 wonder 

8 touch 

9 done 

10 young 

11 ☐☐ ☐ ☐

How did that page go? Choose a face.

'z' sound spelt se

Read each sentence. Draw a line to match it to the best picture.

Please stand in a neat line.

1. You choose the biggest pumpkin of them all.
2. My new blouse is pink and frilly.
3. My headphones make a noise when I turn them on.
4. I raise my hand if I want to speak to the teacher.
5. His older brother likes to tease him sometimes.

Did you do that page with ease?

's' sound spelt se and ce

Look at the picture.
Use the graphemes to make the word.

se or h → h or se

1 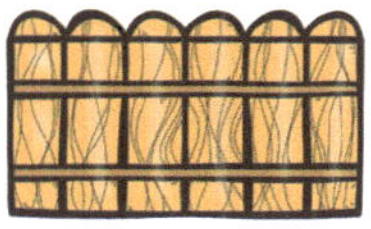 ce e f n

2  ou h se

3  g se oo

4  n ou ce b

5  ur p se

6  ce l f ee

7  r i ce p n

Did you ace this page?

'ee' sound spelt ey

Read the caption.
Colour the best picture
to match each caption.

a monkey

1 push the trolley

2 smoke from a chimney

3 playing hockey

4 some money

5 riding a donkey

6 a turkey with big feathers

Was that page up your alley?

Tricky words

Trace the tricky words.
Then copy the right tricky word to complete each sentence.

| You go | through | the tube. |

thought

through

friend

work

1 | I bounce | ______ | a hoop. |

2 | They | ______ | as a nurse. |

3 | She loves her best | ______ | . |

4 | Hailey | ______ | about |
| other books she wanted to read. |

Did you make light work of that page?

Mixed practice

Read the sentence. Then write it on the dotted line.

Touch the drum to make a noise.

Touch the drum to make a noise.

1. The jockey rides a horse.

....

2. The mother and son bounce.

....

3. My niece Riley welcomes me.

....

4. A young mouse nibbles cheese.

....

How was that page? Colour a face.

‘oo’ and ‘yoo’ sounds spelt ui and ou

Read each sentence. Draw a line to match it to the best picture.

Do you want to go on this cruise ship?

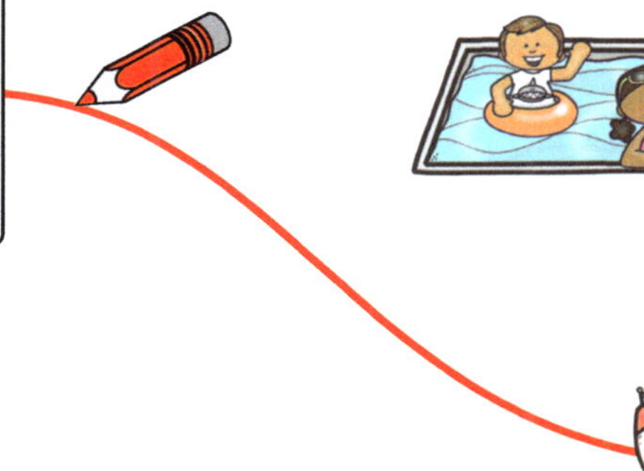

1 This suit goes with my blue boots.

2 The unicorn has a huge fruit.

3 I went to the pool with my youth group.

4 She blew on her soup to cool it.

5 Hassan has a bruise on his leg.

Did you cruise through this page?

'ee' sound recap

Look at the picture.
Use the graphemes to make the word.

ey k

| k | ey |

1  wh l ee

2  air f y

3  o m n ey

4  oo c ie k

5  v n e e

6  f l ea

7 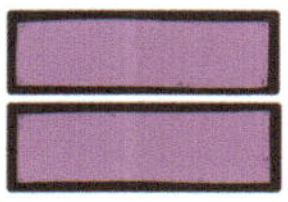 qu e al

Did this page feel easy? Colour a face.

's' and 'z' sound recap

These words either contain the '**z**' sound or the '**s**' sound.
Read the words. Draw lines to show which sound each word contains.

prize

4 buzzing

'z' sound

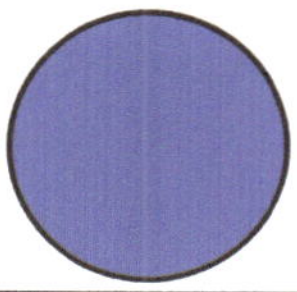

1 circle

5 horse

2 messy

's' sound

6 poison

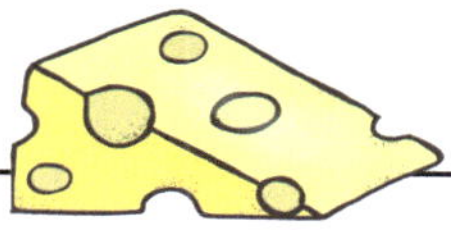

3 cheese

7 fence

Was this page a success? Choose a face.

'oa' sound recap

Read the sentence.
Underline all the graphemes that make the '**oa**' sound.

I hope I can stroke that goat.

1. Jo goes home on the coach.

2. Row a boat to the boulder.

3. This coat is so long that it touches my toes.

4. A slow toad goes up the slope.

5. I have bows on my shoulders.

6. The snow froze my roast.

How did that '**oa**' sound practice go?

Half-term recap

Read the word. Then draw a line to match it to the rhyming word.

Remember that different graphemes can make the same sound.

		soup	petal	
1		kettle	shed	
2		throws	scoop	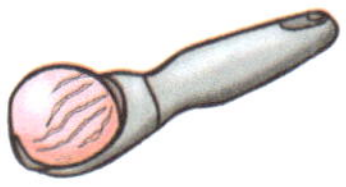
3	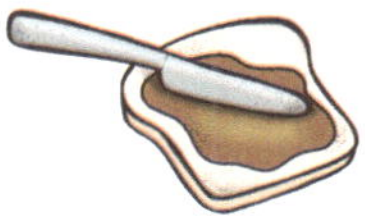	spread	toes	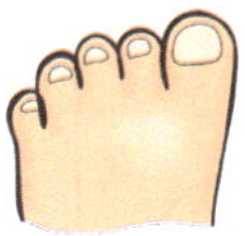
4		worry	flute	
5		suit	folder	
6		shoulder	hurry	

Did you fly through this page?

Half-term recap

Read each sentence. Draw a line to match it to the best picture.

The purple pony can bounce through the window.

1 Joe took a photo of a group of tiny donkeys.

2 Phil gives the prince two magic gems.

3 My brother goes to school with his friend Tracy.

4 You must not touch my piece of gingerbread.

5 The mice eat a whole slice of cheese and some fruit.

How did that go? Colour a face.

Half-term recap

Read the sentence.
Then write it on
the dotted line.

Why is the goose in my trolley?

Why is the goose in my trolley?

(1) The horse thought it could fly.

(2) Has the mouse got whiskers?

(3) I try on a different blouse.

(4) Who can lift a heavy feather?

Are you pleased with how that went?

'ur' sound spelt or

Read the words.
Draw a line to match each word to the best picture.

work

cork

1

words

horns

2

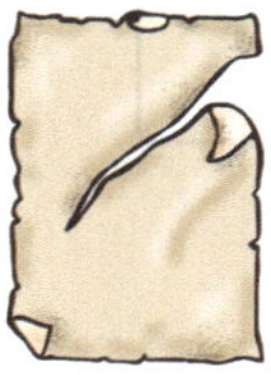

torn

worm

3

horse

world

4

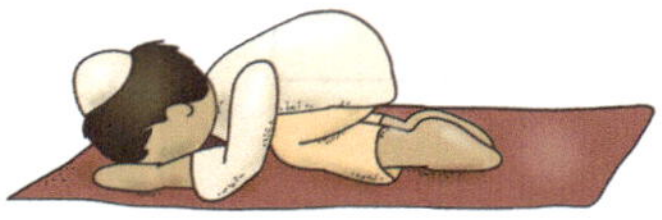

worship

perform

Was that worth a smile? Colour a face.

'oo' sound spelt u and oul

Read the question.
Then tick the box next to the correct answer.

Is it full?

yes ☐
no ☑

1. Did she put a full box by the bush?

yes ☐
no ☐

2. How do you think the bull feels?

joyful ☐
fearful ☐

3. Who could carry the most?

an octopus ☐
a snake ☐

4. What should they do to win?

push ☐
pull ☐

5. Would she like some pudding?

yes ☐
no ☐

Was this page joyful or painful?

'air' sound spelt are

Look at the picture.
Colour the caption that matches the picture.

dare to jump

compare the petals

1 

a brown hare | a rare donkey

2 

glare at whales | care for birds

3 

a spare purse | a bad nightmare

4 

beetles scare me | we are careful

5 

a barefoot girl | a square painting

Colour a face to share how you got on.

'or' sound spelt au, aur, oor and al

Read the sentence.
Underline all the graphemes that make the '**or**' sound.

The author is indoors.

1. I walk outdoors.

2. It is a talking dinosaur.

3. I pause the rocket launch.

4. Claud dropped the chalk on the floor and caused a mess.

5. Paul walks through the door.

6. It haunts the first floor.

Did this page cause you joy?

Tricky words

Trace the tricky words.
Then copy the right tricky word to complete each sentence.

I tried an awful		
sauce	once	.

once   laugh

1 I [   ] at the playful hare.

2 I [   ] saw a rare worm.

3 Jo and Maud did not [   ] when the dinosaur scared them.

4 Mrs Moor asked Saul to stop talking at [   ] .

Was that page a laugh or was it tricky?

Mixed practice

Read each sentence. Draw a line to match it to the best picture.

They should not laugh at poor Clare.

1 I stare at the dinosaur in the laundry room.

2 Please could you share the sauce?

3 Push the button once to pause the ride.

4 The mess was awful and it made him feel worse.

5 He would like to walk around the world in August.

How did you get on with this page?

'ch' sound spelt tch

Look at the picture.
Colour the word that matches the picture.

patch | hatch

1.  witch | ditch

2.  snatch | stretch

3.  catch | crutch

4.  scratch | batch

5. 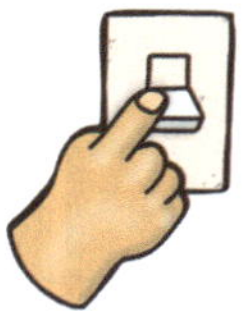 stitch | switch

6.  butcher | fetching

7.  sketching | kitchen

Were you a match for that page?

‘ch’ sound spelt ture

Read the word.
Circle the best picture to match the word.

capture

1 nature

2 mixture

3 picture

4 sculpture

5 creatures

6 furniture

Are you feeling like a champion?

'ar' sound spelt al

Read the sentence.
Then write it on
the dotted line.

The girl is calm.

The girl is calm.

1 The apple is chopped in half.

....

2 She rests by the palm trees.

....

3 You use the blue lip balm.

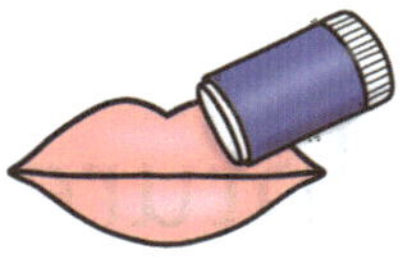

....

4 I saw a newborn calf today.

....

Are you feeling calm after that page?

'ar' sound spelt a

Look at the picture.
Colour the caption that matches the picture.

rather happy	rather sleepy

1 

her father	her class

2 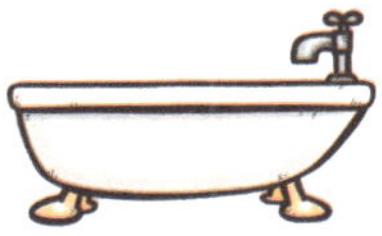

a path	the bath

3 

sprinting very fast	spotting her plants

4 

boy holding a glass	boy with glasses

5 

a mask with feathers	a flask of hot coffee

Are you rather pleased with that page?

Tricky words

Trace the tricky words.
Then copy the right tricky word to complete each sentence.

I shut an eye to wink.

because eye

1. I feel calm ______ I am spending time in nature.

2. Mitch has an ______ test.

3. He has a patch on his ______ .

4. My father put me on his shoulders ______ I could not see.

Did you hit the bullseye on this page?

Mixed practice

Read each sentence. Draw a line to match it to the best picture.

I stitch a patch on my jeans.

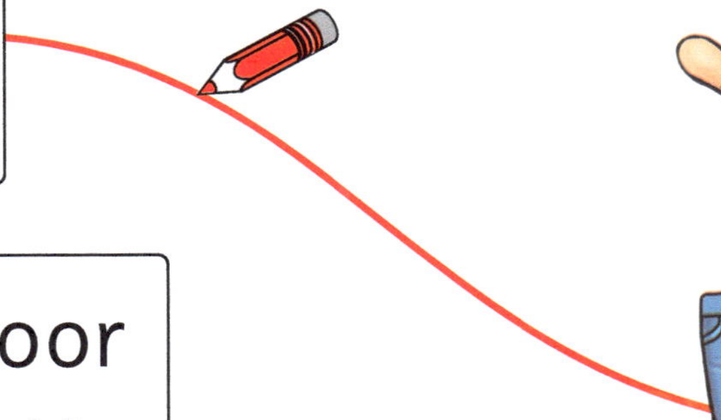

1. He sits on the floor to stretch his calf.

2. A creature crawls on the palm of my hand.

3. A girl in sunglasses points at the water feature.

4. The rabbit hutch is on the grass.

5. Ritchie and I go on an adventure.

How did you find that? Colour a face.

'or' sound spelt a

Read the caption.
Circle the best picture to match the caption.

a brick wall

1. make a call

2. always playing football

3. had a fall

4. a small creature

5. set up a stall

6. almost at the waterfall

Are you feeling tall after that page?

‘uh’ sound in longer words

Look at the picture.
Colour the word that
matches the picture.

lemonade | daffodil

1  flamingo | buffalo

2  fantasy | photograph

3  potato | tomato

4  caravan | caramel

5  dragonfly | difficult

6 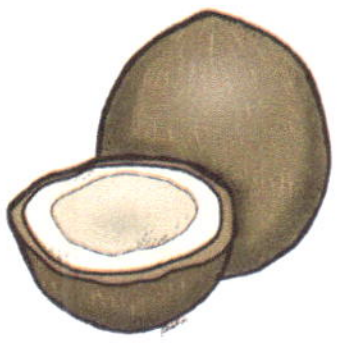 coconut | customer

7  instrument | support

Was that page excellent? Colour a face.

'o' sound spelt a

Read the word in the box.

Tick the word where the grapheme **a** makes the same sound as it does in the word in the box.

squad — swap ☑ — crash ☐

1.  washing

water ☐ 

waffles ☐ 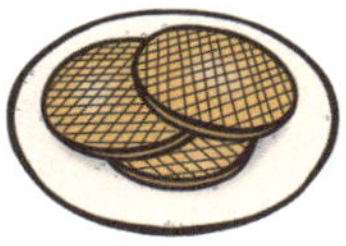

2.  swan

wander ☐ 

strap ☐ 

3.  wand

salt ☐ 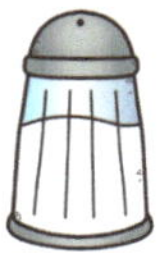

sand ☐ 

4.  watching

dance ☐ 

wasp ☐ 

What did you think of this page?

'air' sound spelt ear and ere

Look at the picture.
Circle the caption that matches the picture.

they swear | they glare

1 

a whole pear | a huge scare

2 

a hairy bear | a tall staircase

3 

tear the paper | repair the furniture

4 

share a pudding | wear a shirt

5 

she put it over there | she asks where it is

Do you feel fairly good about this page?

Mixed practice

Read the question.
Then tick the box next to the correct answer.

Is there a tear in the shirt?

yes ☐
no ☑

1 What do they all play with?

beach balls ☐
magic wands ☐

2 Where is the bear wandering?

on a wall ☐
by a tree ☐

3 Is the kangaroo the tallest animal there?

yes ☐
no ☐

4 Where do they wear a watch?

on their leg ☐
on their arm ☐

5 How many small ducks waddle by the water?

three ☐
five ☐

How did you get on with this page?

‘ur’ sound spelt ear

Read the words.

Colour the word where the grapheme **ear** makes the ‘ur’ sound.

pearl

fear

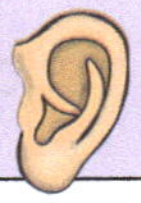
ear

1

search

gear

spear

2

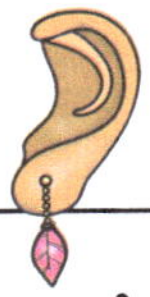
earring

earth

near

3

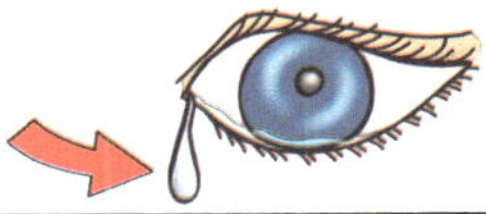
tear

beard

learn

4

shear

research

hear

5

heard

smear

clear

How do you think this page went?

‘r’ sound spelt wr

Read the word.
Circle the best picture to match the word.

write

1 wrist

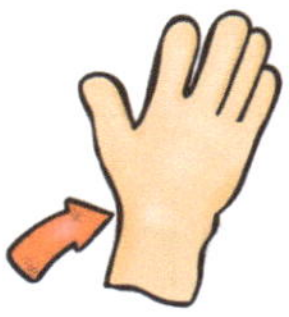

2 wreath

3 wreck

4 wrapping

5 wrong

6 wrinkle

How did that go? Colour in a face.

's' sound spelt st and sc

Read each sentence. Draw a line to match it to the best picture.

He is a science teacher.

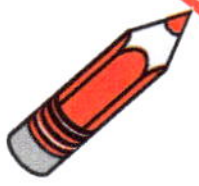

1. The slice of cake has a sweet scent.

2. We sit and listen to the amazing singer.

3. The snail is at the fancy castle with the prince.

4. Wrestling makes her muscles stronger.

5. My friend blows the whistle to start the race.

Are you feeling happy with this page?

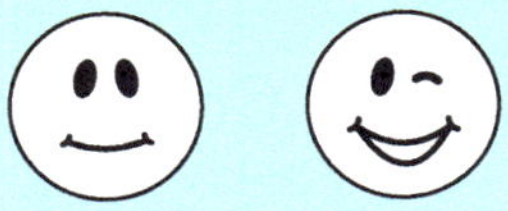

'uh' sound at the end of words

Read the word.
Circle the best picture
to match the word.

sailor

1 tractor

2 collar

3 calendar

4 doctor

5 armour

6 caterpillar

Colour a face to show how you got on.

Mixed practice

Read the sentence.
Then write it on
the dotted line.

That is a muscle.

That is a muscle.

1 The wrap has a spicy flavour.

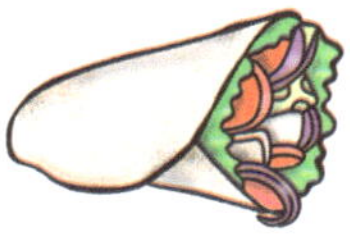

....

2 I am listening to the rehearsal.

....

3 He earns money as an actor.

....

4 The writer is up early today.

....

Was this page great? Colour a face.

'c' and 'sh' sounds spelt ch

In these words, the grapheme **ch** makes either the 'c' sound or the '**sh**' sound. Read the words. Draw lines to show which sound **ch** makes in each one.

anchor

4 Christmas

1 stomach

'c' sound

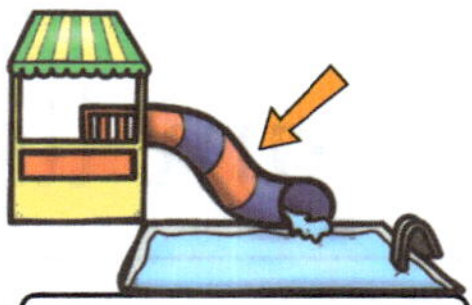

5 chute

2 mechanic

'sh' sound

6 school

3 parachute

7 chef

How did you find that? Colour a face.

's' and 'z' sounds recap

Read each word.
Tick the word that contains the same sound as the grapheme in red.

whisk

mice	✔
daze	

1  dizzy

kiss		
bruise		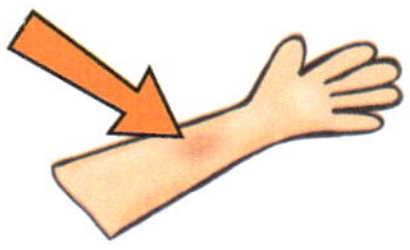

2  cinema

cross		
fizzy		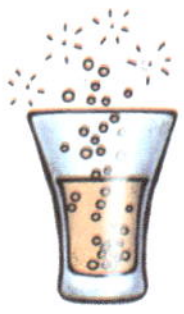

3 

sneeze

snail		
noisy		

4  moose

juice		
freeze		

Do you deserve a round of applause?

‘o’, ‘ar’, ‘or’ and ‘ai’ sounds spelt a

Read the words.
Draw a line to match each word to the best picture.

wasp

fall

1 

call

watch

2 

father

baker

3 

skating

washing

4 

snowball

birdbath

Did you think that page was a blast?

Longer words

Read each sentence. Draw a line to match it to the best picture.

We celebrate in the kitchen.

1 My family is important to me.

2 I think the octopus is an amazing animal.

3 The customer would like a pear.

4 There is a camel in the garden.

5 The driver takes me to the hospital.

How did you find those longer words?

Longer words

Read the question.
Then tick the box next to the correct answer.

Where is the newspaper?

- inside ☑
- outside ☐

1. What size is the elephant?

- gigantic ☐
- small ☐

2. Which person is magical?

- a sailor ☐
- a wizard ☐

3. Are the children whispering quietly?

- yes ☐
- no ☐

4. What is creeping in the tunnel?

- caterpillar ☐
- beetle ☐

5. Was the joyful runner successful in his race?

- yes ☐
- no ☐

Were you triumphant on this page?

Spring term recap

Read the sentence.
Then write it on the dotted line.

The doctor wears a mask.

The doctor wears a mask.

1. I learn to write words at school.

....

2. The calm princess had a snooze.

....

3. I went to dance rehearsal once.

....

4. We could watch the author talk.

....

Did this page make you celebrate?

Spring term recap

Read each sentence. Draw a line to match it to the best picture.

Jun walks from the castle to the kingdom.

1 There is a square picture of a small calf.

2 I sit on the floor to stare at the squad of camels.

3 The smell of food always makes the dog joyful.

4 The green dinosaur has a parachute.

5 The earthworm wriggles in the patch of dirt.

How do you think this recap went?

EOLWSP11